where to lay your weary head

Rest up, relax and recharge

CACHET BOUTIQUE

Sophisticated modernity inside a heritage building

931 Nanjing Xi (West) Lu (at Taixing Lu) / 南京西路931号
(入口在泰兴路) / +86 21 6217 9000 / cachethotels.com

Double from 1,250元

Don't let the fact that it's off a busy street worry you: Cachet Boutique's interior is pin-drop quiet. The handsome stone building was constructed in the 1920s but the rooms are certainly 21st century, with ultra plush beds, dark wood floors, sunburst-printed rugs and a different piece of contemporary Chinese art in every room. Because it is so small, this hotel feels more like serviced flats, complete with a staff who will make sure your stay is personalized without being intrusive – think complimentary afternoon tea and happy hour. It's perfect for travelers who want a home away from home, especially one that comes with attentive service!

LES SUITES ORIENT

Taiwainese hospitality on the Bund

1 Jinling Dong (East) Lu (near Zhongshan Nan (South) Er Lu) / 金陵东路1号
(近中山南二路) / +86 21 6320 0088 / suitesorient.com

Double from 1,470元

If comfort is what you're looking for, then book a room at Les Suites Orient.
Though there are 168 rooms in this building that dates to the 1860s, the staff
members all seem to magically know every guest's name and preferences.
The high-tech room key cards double as Shanghai transportation cards, which
can be used on the metro, ferries, buses and in taxis, but do note that you'll
need to load them with money. Using a digital panel next to the bed, you can
do everything from calling housekeeping to lowering the shades.
Whether you're a night owl or up with the sun, you'll be glad to know
that the lounge, where you can sip coffee or tea, is conveniently open
around the clock.

THE PULI HOTEL AND SPA

Shanghai's sleekest place to sleep

1 Changde Lu (near Nanjing Xi (West) Lu) / 常德路1号 (近南京西路)
+86 21 3203 9999 / thepuli.com

Double from 1,600元

Favored by creative types, this Jing'an hotel's design is a feast of textures.
Local timber, bronze, air-dried clay tiles and reclaimed gray brick were
all used in its construction. There are 250 rooms here, but the hotel
feels much smaller thanks to intimate spaces like the library, which
features stingray leather panels. Its reception desk doubles as a bar, called
The Long Bar, and so named because the teak counter is 100 feet long.
You can check in here and then settle in for a tipple; the lobby is prime
territory for people-watching.

THE WATERHOUSE AT SOUTH BUND

Stripped down luxury

1–3 Maojiayuan Lu (near Waima Lu) / 毛家园路1–3号楼 (近外马路)
+86 21 6080 2988 / waterhouseshanghai.com

Double from 1,350元

Starchitects Neri & Hu broke the hotel mold when they designed this 19-room boutique gem, which ushered in the industrial chic trend that's now seen all over Shanghai. It was a Japanese military base in the 1930s and much of the concrete and brickwork is original to the building. The rooms, spread out over four floors, look like a designer's minimalist pad, complete with mid-century-inspired furniture. In the lobby hangs a Tracy Emin neon light sculpture, an anachronistic touch that feels whimsical amongst all the gray concrete. The hotel also features two bars: one on the roof, the other in the lobby, and the in-house restaurant is the swoonworthy Table No. 1 (see pg 118).

URBN HOTEL SHANGHAI
The greenest retreat
183 Jiaozhou Lu (near Beijing Xi (West) Lu) / 胶州路183号(近北京西路)
+86 21 5153 4600 / urbnhotels.com
Double from 1,280元

China's only carbon-neutral hotel, URBN Hotel Shanghai puts its money where its mouth is. It was built using locally sourced recycled materials, boasts a carbon credits program that supports clean energy projects across China, features an on-site water filtration system and uses only environmentally friendly cleaning products. The 26 rooms are furnished simply, but swankily, with comfortable platform beds and cushy bench seating. A calming color palette of earth tones is used throughout the hotel, giving the impression of a verdant escape, even though it's located in the city. If you want eco-conscious luxury, this is where you'll find it.

jing'an

This neighborhood, so named for Jing'an Temple (which you'll see outside its eponymous metro stop) is where old and new stand side by side. Lane house communities where laundry hangs out to dry on bamboo poles sit a stone's throw from office towers and luxury shops. Following the first Opium War, when the British defeated the Chinese and Shanghai became a foreign treaty port, part of Jing'an was once within the UK and the US's joint International Settlement. Aside from the handful of colonial-style residences, walking through Jing'an today, you'd never know it was once home to a huge number of foreigners.

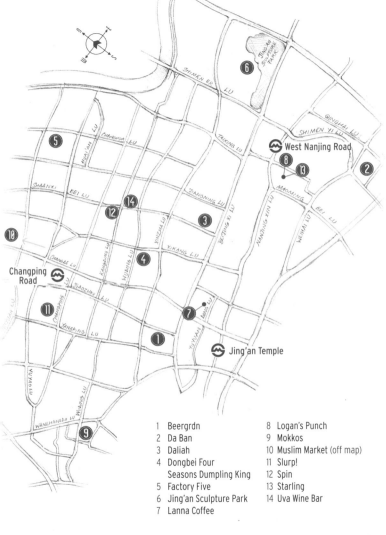

1 Beergrdn
2 Da Ban
3 Daliah
4 Dongbei Four
   Seasons Dumpling King
5 Factory Five
6 Jing'an Sculpture Park
7 Lanna Coffee

8 Logan's Punch
9 Mokkos
10 Muslim Market (off map)
11 Slurp!
12 Spin
13 Starling
14 Uva Wine Bar

BEERGRDN

Casual but sceney pub

183 Jiaozhou Lu (near Xinzha Lu) / 胶州路183号 (近新闸路)
+86 21 5172 1300 / beergrdn.cn / Open daily

Contrary to its name, Beergrdn is actually a gastropub as well as the in-house restaurant at URBN Hotel Shanghai (see pg 9) with a laid-back atmosphere and one of the most tranquil patios in town: since there's free Wi-Fi, you can often find me working outside here, being productive while also enjoying the day and a beverage. The owners have partnered with a brewer in Chengdu to create two custom brews: the GRDN IPA and the GRDN Busty Wheat. They also offer 50 imported beers by the bottle, including my stand-bys, Brasserie de Silly's Scotch de Silly and Rogue Ales' Dead Guy Ale. Pub grub is better here than average, and you can pair your pint with pizza, paninis, Caprese salad and charcuterie and cheese boards.

DA BAN

An unbeatable treat for your feet

370 Dagu Lu (near Chengdu Lu) / 大沽路370号 (近成都路)
+86 21 6340 0366 / No website / Open daily

Foot massages are nice, but particularly so when they take place in a well-heated room during Shanghai's damp, cold winter. Even nicer, though, are foot massages at Da Ban, where each room has a DVD player setup (conveniently, Da Ban is directly across from a DVD store) and unlimited food is included in the price of a massage. I wouldn't recommend having a full meal here, but the fresh juices and peanut butter on toast hit the spot when you're having your feet rubbed and watching a new release – massages are in 60-minute increments, but you're welcome to stay to finish watching your film. Rooms accommodate up to six people, so invite friends, bring a movie and make it a party!

DALIAH

Austrian cuisine in a mod setting

408 Shaanxi Bei (North) Lu (near Beijing Xi (West) Lu)
陕西北路408号 (近北京西路) / **+86 21 6288 8773 / No website**
Open daily

Visions of Austria bring to mind snow-capped mountains and cozy cottages, but at Austrian restuarant Daliah, it's quite the opposite: all sharp right angles, concrete, white Eames-inspired chairs and walls of glass windows that fold back to let in the breeze. From the kitchen come small, pretty dishes — I recommend the quinoa with peas and pickles, crispy pulled beef with polenta and tomatoes, and the chocolate granola, yogurt, strawberry and chocolate sorbet. Oh, and if you like a bit of whimsy, Daliah is dog-friendly, has swings for seats and a slide down from the second floor.

DONGBEI FOUR SEASONS DUMPLING KING

Delicious eats from a far-flung part of China

379 Xikang Lu (near Wuding Lu) 西康路379号 (近武定路)
+86 21 6258 3289 / **No website** / **Open daily**

Dongbei, meaning "northeast", is logically the name of the cuisine from the northeast part of China. It's cold up there, so the food is hearty and they take their dumplings seriously. Which brings me to this: if you eat nothing else here, eat these dumplings. They come 18 to an order, which is plenty for one person, and you can order a half-and-half platter of two types of dumplings. I always go for the classic pork and chive, but the mushroom and bok choy are chewy and filling, and my other must-order, the di san xian (stir-fried eggplant, green bell peppers and potatoes) is savory veggie perfection.

FACTORY FIVE

Custom-built bikes

**Unit S1, 667 Changhua Lu
(near Anyuan Lu) / 昌化路667号S1
(近安远路) / +86 21 8555 5644
wearefactoryfive.com / Closed Monday**

Bikes are nothing new in China, but cycling culture of the sort that's found in North America and Europe was non-existent until recently. No matter: Jeff Liu, Drew Bates and Tyler Bowa bonded over their love of biking and formed their own clubhouse, where they sell bikes and organize rides in Shanghai, as well as further afield. Since they started up five years ago, the trio has restored nearly 1,000 vintage Chinese bicycles. Factory Five now builds its own customized fixed-gear and single-speed bikes and also sells accessories. Custom-builds can be as luxe or frills-free as you want them, but it'll cost you; these start from a cool 4,800元 (around US$775). If you're not in the market to buy and just want to pop in and talk shop, there's a stool and a pint of Brewer's Union waiting for you.

Walk among art

Shimen Er Lu (corner of Beijing Xi (West) Lu) 石门二路 (近北京西路)
No phone or website / Open daily

Shanghai has many trees but not much in the way of big green spaces.
Right downtown, though, is Jing'an Sculpture Park, where I love to stroll
on summer evenings. It would be great for a picnic, but there's a strange
rule that prohibits sitting on the grass in parks here. What makes this
particularly notable are the huge sculptures dotted throughout the
110 acres. Look for Belgian artist LPlus1's big white ostrich, appropriately
named *Ostrich Hide and Seek*, Brit Alex Rinsler's *Urban Fox*, a large,
brown metal fox seated atop a red shipping container, and Belgian
Wim Delvoye's *Tour*, a 40-foot tall Gothic-style tower that stood outside
the Peggy Guggenheim Collection during the 2009 Venice Biennale
before it made its way here.

LANNA COFFEE

Homegrown beans take center stage

8 Yuyuan Dong (East) Lu (near Tongren Lu) / 静安区愚园东路8号
（近铜仁路）/ **+86 180 1767 8867** / **lannacoffee.cn** / **Open daily**

While most of the caffeine slingers in Shanghai boasting about the origins
of their beans are bringing them in from abroad, Lanna Coffee
gets theirs from Yunnan province. For the past five years, founder
Bryan Rakphongphairoj and retail director James Oh have been working
with farmers, helping them to establish more eco-friendly processes to
grow high quality beans with deep flavor. It's worked: everything here,
from poured over, French pressed, or syphoned brews to the espresso-
based drinks, is delicious and lovingly crafted. If you're watching your
wallet, you'll be glad to know that drinks here cost much less than at other
coffee shops, thanks to the local beans.

LOGAN'S PUNCH

Rowdy cocktail joint

2nd Floor, 99 Taixing Lu (near Nanjing Xi (West) Lu) / 泰兴路99号2楼
(近南京西路) / **+86 21 6246 5928** / loganspunch.com / **Closed Monday**

This is no sedate lounge where tunes play at a comfortable background
level. Owner Logan Brouse loves himself a good party, so he hosts one every
night. Built inside a turn-of-the-century lane house, Logan's Punch has
two sides: one that's divided into intimate booths with dark brick walls,
and the other, like the courtyards of traditional laneway homes, is open air.
The stereo pumps dance tunes and the team behind the bar mix up huge
punch bowls that are meant to be shared. For a little caffeine boost along
with my alcohol, I go with my pals and order the Emperor Norton Punch –
cinnamon, orgeat syrup, orange cream bitters, white cacao, grapefruit,
Earl Grey tea and, as the menu puts it, "a metric shit ton of tequila".

MOKKOS

Nearly hidden shōchū bar

**1245 Wuding Xi (West) Lu (near Wanhangdu Lu) / 武定西路1245号
(近万航渡路) / +86 21 6212 1114 / No website / Open daily**

Walk slowly along Wuding Xi Lu or you'll miss Mokkos, a barely marked closet-sized bar specializing in shōchū, a Japanese spirit that is distilled, not fermented like sake. (Think whisky vs vodka). The space is small, dark, smoky and there's often reggae on the stereo. When I say it's small, I mean it: there are only four tables, a tightly packed eight seats at the bar and the occasional milk crate turned on end to create an extra seat. The shelves behind the bar are lined with hundreds of shōchū bottles, and there's no menu, so I generally point to what I want, or simply tell the bartender how much I want to spend and let the professional ply me with what he thinks is best.

MUSLIM MARKET

A unique weekly festival of food

Aomen Lu (near Changde Lu) / 澳门路 (近常德路)
No phone or website / Open Friday

Every Friday, Shanghai's population of Uyghur Muslims gathers for this lively market outside Huxi Mosque, the only Muslim market in Shanghai. A word of warning: sometimes the government cracks down and closes the market, though they always re-open it a few days later. There is so much to taste here: fresh yogurt, unbelievable dumplings with fillings such as lamb and pumpkin, perfectly cooked pilaf, ultra-tender lamb skewers, sesame breads right out of the oven, piles of almond cookies and dozens of bins brimming with dried fruit including all manner of raisins. Everything is inexpensive here, with a whole roast chicken going for just 10元 (around US$2). So what I'm saying is, come hungry.

SLURP!

Southern street eats in a colorful space

1000 Changping Lu (near Yanping Lu) / 昌平路1000号 (近延平路)
+86 180 0186 9001 / No website / Closed Monday

At Slurp!, Lei Yu from Guizhou province and Niu Yun from Yunnan
province serve the street-style food they ate as kids. Their restaurant's
interior resembles a bright Melbourne café, not a hole-in-the-wall
in southern China, but that doesn't detract from the authenticity of
the food. Noodle soups are the specialty here, and you can pick your
noodle type: thin mixian or thick ersi, both made of rice. If you like your
soup with a kick, as I do, the Kunming-style xiao guo mixian has garlic,
preserved vegetables and lots of chili peppers. It's salty though; be sure to
wash it down with Dali beer or mugua shui, a sweet drink with papaya,
rose jam and brown sugar.

SPIN

Chinese ceramics to spruce up your home

379 Kangding Lu (near Shaanxi Bei (North) Lu)   康定路379号
（近陕西北路） **+86 21 6279 2545   spinceramics.com   Open daily**

The minute I receive a wedding invitation, I hop on my bike and ride over to Spin. This sleek concrete temple of ceramics sells elegant dinnerware, jewelry and home goods such as pretty soap dispensers and tiny, ceramic dumplings that come in a bamboo steamer. Nearly everything for sale here is white, but some pieces are splashed with bold blue or red brushstrokes. That being said, the piece I love most in the shop is an impeccably detailed white porcelain wutong leaf.

STARLING

Colonial vibes from a team who knows their drinks

99 Taixing Lu (near Nanjing Xi (West) Lu) / 泰兴路99号 (近南京西路)
+86 21 6217 0189 / facebook.com/pages/Starling / Closed Monday

From the editors of China's bar industry magazine *DRiNK* comes this nostalgic cocktail bar. Wanting to bring to Shanghai the ambiance of Rangoon's infamous Pegu Club of yore and Singapore's still-operating Long Bar at Raffles Hotel, the owners have kitted Starling out with a richly patterned tile floor, dark woods and Palisade ceiling fans that whir overhead. It's by no means a true replica of a colonial-era bar, but it's fun nonetheless. Drinks skew a little spring break, but are still tasty. My pick is The Monsoon, a concoction of Grand Marnier, lime, rum, ginger, bitters and curry leaves served in a copper mug.

UVA WINE BAR

Vino and vittles

819 Shaanxi Bei (North) Lu (near Kangding Lu) / 陕西北路819号
(近康定路) / **+86 21 5228 0320** / **uvashanghai.com** / **Open daily**

Piercarlo Panozzo and his partner Ivan Acardi have set up a convivial bar
that lends itself to long conversations. Most of the wine here is of Italian
origin, like the Medici Ermete Lambrusco which I find pleasingly dry.
With filament bulbs casting flattering light over intimate clusters of seats,
Uva (meaning "grape" in Italian, nothing to do with rays) is the ideal local,
and it doesn't leave the beer drinkers feeling left out: they can sip Estrella
and Red Star if they refuse the wine. The kitchen produces tasty pizzas, but
I prefer boards of imported Italian cheese and cured meats to accompany
my glass of red.

i want to ride my bicycle

Cruise through the city

Shanghai is pancake flat, which means that cycling isn't too difficult and is a fun way to get around town. Hire a bike from **Giant** for 50元 (around US$8) per day, or, if you're in town for a little longer, it might make more sense to buy: you can pick up a used bike by browsing the classifieds on Smart Shanghai's website (smartshanghai. com), or, if you're in the market for something custom, swing by Factory Five (see pg 16). Once you've scored yourself a bike, you can embark on three enjoyable rides around the city, all of which are between five and ten kilometers (three and six miles).

Shaded by towering plane trees until the last stretch, the **Fuxing Lu Route** is extremely pleasant, and is perfect for riders who aren't already confident biking in a city. Start at the corner of Fuxing Xi (West) Lu and Wukang Lu in the French Concession, and continue all the way to Fuxing Dong (East) Lu, ending at Madang Lu in Xintiandi. You'll cruise past stately colonial-style homes, wine bar Salute (see pg 72) and Fuxing Park before coming to rest one block south of salad spot Sproutworks (see pg 106). It's a straight shot and you'll be in the safety of the bike lane the whole way.

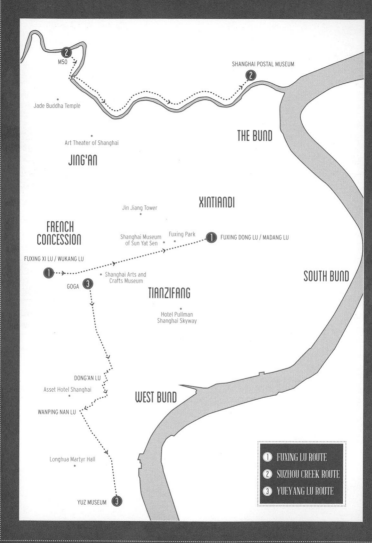

For a trail chock-full of culture, take the **Suzhou Creek Route**: start off in Jing'an at art gallery complex M50, and end in the Bund at Shanghai Postal Museum (see pg 116). This leads you along Suzhou Creek – once the boundary between the British Concession and the American Settlement – towards the Huangpu River. Just before you reach the Bund, dismount at the Shanghai Postal Museum, where admission is free, and head up to the roof deck for great views of the Bund and Pudong skyline. Pro tip: pack a bottle of wine and cups.

The **Yueyang Lu Route**, featuring a ride from the south end of the French Concession to the West Bund, is not for the faint of heart. While safe, there aren't bike lanes throughout and more than half of it is in direct sunlight. Start in the French Concession outside of GoGa (see pg 63), on the corner of Dongping Lu and Yueyang Lu, then head south on Yueyang Lu; at Zhaojiabang Lu, Yueyang turns into Fenglin Lu. Keep going, then turn right at Lingling Lu and left onto on Dong'an Lu. At Longhua Lu, make a slight right and then a left onto Wanping Nan (South) Lu. You'll soon hit Fenggu Lu in the West Bund and end at the Yuz Museum (see pg 124), where you can eye vibrant contemporary Chinese art.

french concession

Yan'an Overpass to Huaihai Zhong Lu

From the south side of the Yan'an Overpass to Huaihai Zhong Lu lies the northern half of the French Concession. During Shanghai's colonial heyday, from 1849 until 1943 – long before the expressway was there – this area was controlled by the French, thus the name. This neighborhood was the go-to for a wild night out, with expats and locals alike toasting to their successes and sorrows in cabaret clubs and cocktail bars. It seems not much has changed in the last century, as it's this area that remains the epicenter of Shanghai cool; on its tree-lined streets – those same trees that shaded playboys and dancing girls during the city's Golden Era – are a slew of trendy bars, restaurants, cafés and shops that beckon all.

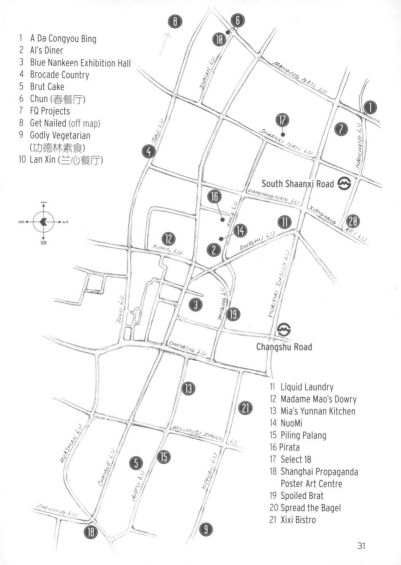

1 A Da Congyou Bing
2 Al's Diner
3 Blue Nankeen Exhibition Hall
4 Brocade Country
5 Brut Cake
6 Chun (春餐厅)
7 FQ Projects
8 Get Nailed (off map)
9 Godly Vegetarian
   (功德林素食)
10 Lan Xin (兰心餐厅)

11 Liquid Laundry
12 Madame Mao's Dowry
13 Mia's Yunnan Kitchen
14 NuoMi
15 Piling Palang
16 Pirata
17 Select 18
18 Shanghai Propaganda
   Poster Art Centre
19 Spoiled Brat
20 Spread the Bagel
21 Xixi Bistro

A DA CONGYOU BING

Scallion pancakes from the master

No. 2, Lane 159 Maoming Nan (South) Lu (near Nanchang Lu)
茂名南路159弄2号 (近南昌路) / **No phone or website**
Closed Wednesday

For six days a week over the past 30 years, Mr Wu has begun his day at the crack of dawn to make congyou bing (scallion pancakes) in his tiny stand. He is a virtuoso of this beloved Chinese breakfast food, and his savory pancakes have such a cult following that the queue often forms before sunrise. Each ball of dough gets a bit of lard, then pork and green onion before being tossed onto the griddle and flattened into a pancake. No congyou bing is served until it's browned and crispy on both sides, at which moment it's slipped into a little brown paper sleeve, and becomes yours to inhale.

AL'S DINER

American comfort food and scrumptious ice cream

204 Xinle Lu (near Donghu Lu) / 新乐路204号 (近东湖路)
+86 21 5465 1259 / eatalalsdiner.com / Open daily

Summer temperatures regularly top 40°C (100°F) in Shanghai. When coupled with the accompanying humidity, it's all I can do to crawl the few blocks from my apartment to Al's Diner. In addition to the menu featuring all-day breakfast, a Monte Cristo and chicken fried steak, the store serves Gracie's Ice Cream, and that is the reason I come here. With a selection of 16 house-made flavors, asking me to pick my favorite would be like picking my favorite child (it's just not done). But I can highly recommend the malt, sea salt and dark chocolate; the black sesame and honey; and the Hokkaido soft serve topped with a chunk of honeycomb. The store offers cups and waffle cones as vessels for the smooth, fist-sized scoops, so pick the one your heart desires and indulge.

BLUE NANKEEN EXHIBITION HALL

Indigo-dyed everything

House 24, Lane 637 Changle Lu (between Fumin Lu and Changshu Lu)
长乐路637弄24室 (富民路和常熟路之间) / **+86 21 5403 7947**
No website / Open daily

In a pale yellow building tucked at the end of a lane is this delightful shop and garden café. Blue nankeen, a handicraft from southern China, is made using stencils and indigo dye to create an intricate pattern that resembles a cross between Japanese katazome and Indonesian batik. Here, you'll find Shanghai's widest array of blue nankeen clothing for men, women and children, as well as bags, hats and adorable soft toys. My recommendation for those who are DIY-inclined are the bright bolts of fabric to fashion into whatever you fancy.

BROCADE COUNTRY

Vibrant Miao textiles

616 Julu Lu (near Xiangyang Bei (North) Lu) / 巨鹿路616
(近襄阳北路) / **+86 21 6279 2677** / **No website** / **Open daily**

Though the Miao in Guizhou, Guangxi and Yunnan provinces live far
from Shanghai, their fashion has become en vogue in the city. Luckily,
Brocade Country is here to fill your home with Miao goods: think Mandarin-
collared jackets, cropped trousers, swirly skirts and tote bags. You'll pay a
dozen times here what you would in the southern countryside, but if you
aren't able to visit the provinces, this is your best bet for authentic garments.
Look for silver jewelry and gorgeous, intricately embroidered textiles that
have been turned into womenswear and accessories. If you're having a hard
time choosing, the textiles themselves, which can double as chic blankets
and tablecloths, are always a great way to go.

BRUT CAKE

Quirky ceramics and home goods

232 Anfu Lu (near Wulumuqi Lu) / 安福路232号 (近乌鲁木齐路)
+86 21 5448 8159 / brutcake.com / Open daily

Inspired by the Art Brut movement, gregarious Taiwanese artist
Nicole Teng created her store's name by combining the word "brut" with
the word "cake," which she feels "evokes images of simple pleasures".
Indeed, her shop is a cheerful place with whimsical handmade ceramics
– functional cups, bowls and plates – filling the shelves. Teng leaves some
pieces unglazed, giving them a pleasingly rustic look, but I always go for
the mugs painted with smiling faces, perfect for an afternoon cuppa.
Larger pieces include light fixtures made from upcycled iron faucets and
reclaimed wooden chairs upholstered in vintage fabrics to create adorable
cartoon faces.

CHUN (春餐厅)

Homey Shanghainese restaurant

124 Jinxian Lu (near Maoming Nan (South) Lu) / 进贤路124号
(近茂名南路) / **+86 21 6256 0301** / **No website** / **Closed Sunday**

This tiny eatery on block-long Jinxian Lu epitomizes the old adage "don't judge a book by its cover". It looks humble, even a little drab, with its four tables, complete lack of décor and no menu in sight. Even so, if you don't make a reservation woe is you because locals flock here in droves for the homestyle food. Chun is essentially the private kitchen of no-nonsense proprietor Lan-Lan; she'll tell you what's available that day and exactly how much to order based on the number of people in your party. Though there's no printed menu, specialties often include pork-stuffed snails, puréed broad beans with Chinese pickles, red-braised duck and steamed river shrimp.

FQ PROJECTS

Hidden laneway art gallery

No. 76, 927 Huaihai Zhong Lu (near Maoming Nan (South) Lu)
淮海中路927弄淮海坊76号 (近茂名南路   +86 21 6466 2940
fqprojects.com | Closed Monday

Venture down a narrow lane just off Huaihai Zhong Lu and you'll find
FQ Projects, a small, lovely gallery. Outside, the scene is classic Shanghai
– an alleyway lined with redbrick lane houses. Within, it's all gleaming
hardwood floors and rotating exhibitions of work by Chinese artists.
Of note on my recent visit here were the pieces by Yang Yongliang,
which are an amalgam of traditional Chinese landscape paintings and
construction scenes from today, as well as Yansha Zian's colorful paintings
of crowds. I was tempted to buy Zian's piece with tiny abstract figures
carrying bright umbrellas, hurrying across a pedestrian scramble; a scene
familiar to anyone who's ever crossed a Shanghai street on a rainy day.

GET NAILED

Tidy little salon

256 Julu Lu (near Maoming Nan (South) Lu) / 巨鹿路256号
(近茂名南路) / **+86 21 5299 0980 / No website / Open daily**

This posh, pint-sized parlor is my choice nail place: it has Wi-Fi and
experienced, English-speaking staff members who provide damn good
manicures and pedicures. What I love most is that they use imported,
organic polishes like Essie, OPI, CND and IBD — no cheap colors with toxic
ingredients here. The manicurists can do everything from a good old-
fashioned pedicure to a longer-lasting gel manicure with artsy designs.
Other services offered are pampering moisture treatments for your hands
and feet, as well as eyelash extensions. Take heed, though: there are
only two recliners here for pedicures and three chairs for manicures,
so appointments are essential.

GODLY VEGETARIAN
(功德林素食)

Where veggies reign supreme

303 Wuyuan Lu (near Wukang Lu) / 五原路303号 (近武康路)
+86 21 6471 8909 / shgodly.com / Open daily

The fact that this neighborhood noodle joint is strictly vegetarian doesn't stop carnivorous souls from pulling up a heavy wooden chair. I always order the plump wontons, which have silky skins and tender greens within, and noodles that are just the right al dente texture. There are also a few mock meat dishes here, like Peking "duck" made of seitan and served with savory pancakes, thinly sliced cucumber and sweet bean sauce. It's a cheap, friendly place right on the corner of a leafy residential street, great for a quick lunch or early dinner.

LAN XIN (兰心餐厅)

Chinese comfort food

**130 Jinxian Lu (near Maoming Nan (South) Lu) / 进贤路130号
(近茂名南路) / +86 21 6253 3554 / No website / Open daily**

Like nearby Chun (see pg 37), Lan Xin has no atmosphere but food so
fantastic that even Cantopop megastar Faye Wong swings by when she's
in town. The faded sign is only in Mandarin and lace curtains hide what's
within, so the tip-off here is the queue of hungry locals and handful of
luxury cars idling out front. Under fluorescent lights, diners seated at one
of six tables tuck into Shanghai classics like hongshao rou (red braised
pork), wok-fried river shrimp, bamboo shoot soup and scallions with
scrambled eggs. There's no English menu, so just point to what looks good
on other tables and rest easy knowing that you really can't go wrong here.

LIQUID LAUNDRY

New York-inspired gastropub

2nd Floor, 1028 Huaihai Zhong Lu (near Donghu Lu)
淮海中路1028号, 嘉华房2楼 (近东湖路) / **+86 21 6445 9589**
theliquidlaundry.com / **Open daily**

If you're looking for somewhere trendy and upscale to dine, drink and dance, head here on a Friday or Saturday night. Pizzas fly out of the behemoth oven in the corner of the subway-tiled, industrial space lit by exposed Edison bulbs, as a DJ spins and the social media savvy clientele snap photos before digging into the well-plated beef tongue sliders, pork trotter croquettes and slices of seared yellowtail topped with pumpkin, pear, pine nuts, puffed black rice, avocado and sliced jalapeños. Into microbrews? Liquid Laundry's North American owners also run Boxing Cat brewery and a rotating selection of their craft beers, like the malty TKO IPA, are always on tap.

MADAME MAO'S DOWRY

Chinoiserie gone kitsch

207 Fumin Lu (near Julu Lu) / 富民路207号 (近巨鹿路)
+86 21 5403 3551 / madamemaosdowry.org / Open daily

Walking down Fumin Lu, you'll recognize Madame Mao's Dowry by
its cornflower blue façade. British owner Linda Johnson has a keen eye
and fills her shop with whatever she fancies, from authentic
Communist Era propaganda art posters — at prices that are very much
capitalist — to goods from young local designers. Look for baozi-printed
dishtowels and dinnerware from Pinyin Press (see pg 53), Paper Tiger's
eco-friendly wrapping paper (I fancy the Bund print; see page 55) and
Grifted's cheery necklaces made from candy wrappers and paper clips.
I live only five blocks from this store, and it's my go-to for gifts that say
"uniquely made in China" rather than those that scream "schlock from the
tourist market".

MIA'S YUNNAN KITCHEN

Cheap and cheerful southern eats

45 Anfu Lu (near Changshu Lu) / 安福路45号 (近常熟路)
+86 21 5403 5266 / No website / Open daily

With vegetarian dishes and nothing on the menu to make you squeamish,
Mia's Yunnan Kitchen is the first place I bring Middle Kingdom newbies.
Yes, Shanghai is known for xiaolongbao (soup dumplings), and here I am
sending you to eat cuisine from a province 1,430 miles southwest. But the
salt-and-pepper coated pan-fried goat cheese is moreish, the spicy mint
salad refreshing and the heaping plate of pickled mashed potatoes the ideal
stomach-liner. I can't help but love the simple, rough-hewn wooden tables,
and the fact that the restaurant doesn't have Wi-Fi, allowing you to take a
break from your phone and make conversation with your dining companions.

NUOMI

Clothing that gives back

196 Xinle Lu (near Donghu Lu) / 新乐路196号 (近东湖路)
+86 21 5403 4199 / nuomishanghai.com / Open daily

From the street, NuoMi appears to be nothing more than a boutique selling Asian-influenced women's and childrenswear in cotton, bamboo, cashmere and silk. If all you're looking for is beautiful clothing, then you can pop in, buy a few things and be on your merry way. What I love most about this store is that it's committed to being socially responsible. The retail arm of BrownRice Designs, which works with disadvantaged locals to provide them with job skills, the store's designers teach these individuals to sew, providing much-needed income for those who would otherwise be unable to support themselves and their families. When you shop here, you know that you're supporting fair trade and local artisans, which always makes me leave with an extra bounce in my step.

PILING PALANG

Gleeful contemporary ceramics

183 Anfu Lu (near Wulumuqi Lu) / 安福路183号（常熟路和乌鲁木齐路之间）
+86 21 6422 7577 / **pilingpalang.com/en** / **Open daily**

Tianjin-born-and-raised Deng Bingbing spent 10 years working as a graphic designer in Melbourne before moving to Shanghai and starting his own company – Piling Palang, one of my most frequented shops in Shanghai. Deng expertly combines Chinese and Western aesthetics into his brightly colored ceramics. The pieces can properly be called objets d'art and they're finished in lacquer, ceramic and cloisonné. Ceramic trays printed with 1930s Shanghai signboards make excellent, moderately priced souvenirs, as do the cups and small plates printed with acrobats. The most expensive of the lot are the cloisonné, but the work is exquisite and worth the splurge.

PIRATA

Fantastic small plates

136 Xinle Lu (near Xiangyang Bei (North) Lu)
徐汇区新乐路136号（近襄阳北路） / **+86 21 5404 2327**
No website / Closed Monday

Shanghai's persnickety chefs pour into this tapas kitchen for post-shift, late night bites and draft Asahi – a sure sign that the food's up to par. On chef Ling Huang's menu are assorted plates that range from simple beef kebabs fragranced with onion and coriander served atop pita, to garlicky shrimp scampi a la plancha, to fried mini calamari. The squid, delivered on a wooden cutting board, are addictively crunchy and are served with fried basil leaves and a light mayonnaise. I have to remind myself every time not to fill up entirely on the savory, as dessert here – praline ice cream rolled in crushed peanuts and then wrapped in coriander and a crêpe – is not to be missed.

SELECT 18

A treasure trove of clothing, décor and rare finds

No. 96, Lane 39 Shaanxi Nan (South) Lu (near Xinle Lu)
陕西南路39弄96号 (近新乐路) / **No phone**
facebook.com/select18 / Open daily

Alex Rolfe and her business partner Thomas Lee have turned the ground floor of a 1920s lane house into a cute multi-concept shop that stocks new and pre-loved clothing, as well as décor. It's mostly independent designers featured here, with clothing from labels such as Whillas & Gun, Ross & Brown and The Hat Lab, and upcycled home goods by Jonas' Design (see pg 55). On the vintage side are cufflinks, statement hats from Hong Kong's Jaycow Millinery, My Babouche brand Moroccan slippers and high-end jewelry – think Dior, Cartier and Chanel – that will tempt you to break the bank every time you set foot inside.

SHANGHAI PROPAGANDA POSTER ART CENTRE

Workers of the world, unite!

Basement, Block B, 868 Huashan Lu (near Zhenning Lu)
华山路868号B号楼（近镇宁路）/ +86 21 6211 1845
shanghaipropagandaart.com / Open daily

In the basement of a residential tower is this museum whose drab exterior belies the gems within. Yang Pei Ming has been collecting Chinese propaganda posters since 1995; today, his museum houses a whopping 6,000 posters produced between 1940 and 1990, as well as an impressive collection of Shanghai Lady pin-up calendars from the early 20th century. There's also Cultural Revolution-era ephemera, like used copies of Mao's *Little Red Book*, ration tokens and household goods with slogans like "serve the people". If you're into communist kitsch, this is the place to come for a proper dose of it.

SPOILED BRAT

Delicate handmade jewelry

No. 6, Lane 123 Yanqing Lu (near Huating Lu) / 延庆路123弄6号 (近华亭路) / **+86 21 3668 1567** / **spoiledbratjewelry.com** / **Open daily**

Steffie Wu started her jewelry business in Los Angeles, making a name for herself there before opening her only boutique in Shanghai, a Cali-inspired space with a teal accent wall, plants in bell jars and jewelry displayed on mossy circles. Each piece of Wu's jewelry is made by hand and one-of-a-kind: she sources semi-precious stones and pairs the colorful gems with sterling silver and 14-carat gold. Earrings start at 300元 (around US$50), but a thriftier option is the "lucky color bracelet"; decorated with silver charms, it's traditionally believed that the five colors of these strings bring good luck: green for wealth, red for love, purple for friendship, yellow for enhanced spirituality and blue for a long life.

50

SPREAD THE BAGEL
New York flavor with global appeal

611 Nanchang Lu (near Xiangyang Lu) / 南昌路611号 (近襄阳路)
+86 136 6162 1328 / spreadthebagel.com / Open daily

Leave it not to a New Yorker, but to an enterprising Californian to bring bagels to Shanghai. Christine Asuncion got her start making the iconic treat at home in her tiny oven and delivering them. Word spread and the overwhelming demand led to her own storefront, where people pour in all day to nosh on the chewy bagels Christine and her local team pump out. As a New York native, I always go right for the classic schmear and lox on an everything bagel, but, if that's not your jam, there's also a short list of delicious bagel sandwiches and nine other kinds of bagels, including the unorthodox El Jalapeño Cheddar.

XIXI BISTRO

Chinese-Italian fusion in a 1930s villa

89 Wuyuan Lu (near Wulumuqi Lu) / 五原路89号 (近乌鲁木齐路)
+86 21 6486 1331 / No website / Open daily

When a pair of Italians got their hands on a 1930s lane house situated on a quiet street, they got to work converting it into their dream space: a first-floor restaurant with polished hardwood floors, sumptuous wallpaper and Art Deco-inspired ceiling lamps that provide lighting low enough for dates but not too romantic for business dinners, a second-floor cocktail bar and backyard garden. The food is Italian-Chinese fusion, and my picks are the spinach, mozzarella and pine nut guotie (pan-fried dumplings), ricotta with deep-fried mantou (steamed bun) and traditional Shanghainese congyou banmian (scallion oil noodles) gussied up with Alaskan pollock roe.

made in china

Locally crafted souvenirs that will impress

"Made in China" tends to have a negative connotation, but these four designers are smashing that stereotype. Their Shanghai-inspired goods can be bought directly, or found at boutiques throughout the city: check out Madame Mao's Dowry (see pg 43) as well as Select 18 (see pg 48) to pick up some of these pretties.

Pinyin Press began with a line of Sarah Armstrong's illustrated note cards and tote bags. The totes have a cult following, and you'll see them on shoulders all over the city. Sarah's collection, sold at Madame Mao's Dowry (see pg 43) as well as other Shanghai boutiques, has expanded and now includes tea towels pretty enough to frame, coasters and bone china mugs emblazoned with symbols that are recognizably representative of China, such as dumplings, baozi (steamed buns) and zodiac signs.

PINYIN PRESS

CUKIMBER

PAPER TIGER

JONAS' DESIGN

CUKIMBER
No address, +86 150 0042 3954, cukimber.com

JONAS' DESIGN
Building 15, Wuwei Creative Garden, 1436 Jungong Lu
(near Xiangyin Lu), 军工路1436号五维创意园区
15栋 (近翔殷路), +86 134 7275 4027
jonasdesign.net

PAPER TIGER
No address or phone, papertigershanghai.com

PINYIN PRESS
No address, +86 137 6195 9244, pinyinpress.com

The woman behind **Cukimber**, Kimberly Wong, creates handmade earrings and necklaces in wavy, organic shapes. She sources the thin metal from a local vendor and picks up beads and other supplies here, in New York and on her global travels. Custom pieces start from 300元 (around US$50) and take two weeks to make, but can be shipped worldwide.

When Lucy Young moved from New York to Shanghai, she was surprised to find there was nowhere to buy wrapping paper. The idea for **Paper Tiger**, then, was simple: create and sell beautiful, sustainable giftwrap. The designs are inspired by what Lucy sees living in Shanghai, but she also works with other artists, like Beijing resident Steffi Hanson, who designed the Peking Opera print. The paper is so pretty that it makes a great gift on its own – be sure to pick some up when you visit Madame Mao's Dowry (see pg 43).

Working out of a studio in northern Shanghai, you'll find Jonas Merian of **Jonas' Design** repurposing used local products to build unique furniture and home goods. He turns colorful biscuit tins into speakers, transforms kettles into ceiling lamps and upcycles bright rotary telephones into clocks. His designs, which you can purchase by visiting him at his studio or by swinging by Select 18 (see pg 48), are a great way to grab a quirky piece of décor and take a little bit of Shanghai home with you.

french concession

Huaihai Zhong Lu to Zhaojiabang Lu

The southern half of the French Concession was prime territory for foreigners for nearly a century, which is evident from the minute you hit this neighborhood's pavement – with narrow streets shaded by towering plane trees, you immediately feel as if you've been transported out of Shanghai and into Europe. The streets are lined in a mix of handsome English and French architecture juxtaposed against more traditional Chinese styles, and many embassies are based here, housed in stately villas, giving this area the feeling of multicultural glamour. From a place to play French pastime pétanque to Shanghai's only screen-printing studio to traditional tea houses, here's where to go.

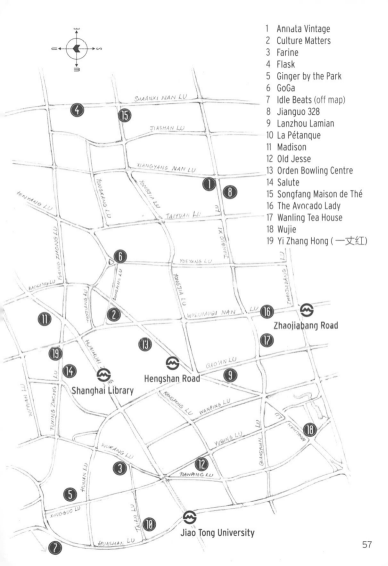

1 Annata Vintage
2 Culture Matters
3 Farine
4 Flask
5 Ginger by the Park
6 GoGa
7 Idle Beats (off map)
8 Jianguo 328
9 Lanzhou Lamian
10 La Pétanque
11 Madison
12 Old Jesse
13 Orden Bowling Centre
14 Salute
15 Songfang Maison de Thé
16 The Avocado Lady
17 Wanling Tea House
18 Wujie
19 Yi Zhang Hong (一丈红)

ANNATA VINTAGE

Selectively curated goods

No. 23, Lane 316 Jianguo Xi (West) Lu (near Xiangyang Nan (South) Lu) / 建国西路316弄23号楼 (近襄阳南路) / +86 136 3641 8880
No website / Closed Monday

When Ting Zhang and Julia Jameson met at a dinner party, they bonded over their shared love of all things vintage. Soon, they banded together to open this little shop, whose name means "vintage year" in Italian. The store is a mini-UN of throwback finds, with French and British hats dating from the 1950s, '70s and '80s-style blouses and dresses found in Holland and Japan, and jewelry picked up in Turkey, Italy and England. Prices vary, with items like coin purses and tea dresses on the more inexpensive end, and rarer finds, like a pair of Mary Janes from the 1920s (nearly a century old!) priced to match their age.

Retro Shanghai kicks

15 Dongping Lu (near Hengshan Lu)   东平路15号 (近衡山路)
+86 136 7188 2040   facebook.com/shtianbo   Open daily

This closet-sized sneaker shop is the place to go if you're in the market for
a pair of Feiyues. Inspired by the shoes worn by Shaolin monks, the brand,
which features rubber soles and canvas uppers, was born in Shanghai in
the late 1950s. Originally, the shoes were only available in white and black,
but today you'll find them in a range of colors and cuts, though the classic
white low-tops remain my choice. Feiyues start from just 50元 (around
US$8), though you can pay a bit more to have your pair customized with
anything from your initials to I ❤ SH to graffiti-style designs.

FARINE

Parisian confections worth the splurge

378 Wukang Lu (near Tai'an Lu) / 武康路378号 (近泰安路)
+86 21 6126 7661 / farine-bakery.com / Open daily

Franck Pecol is a Frenchman, a chef and a keen eater who is intent on bringing the cuisine of France to Shanghai. His bakery, Farine, channels Paris with slick subway tiles, reclaimed wood and a charming chalkboard menu. Take heed, though: this is Shanghai's most expensive bakery, but also its best. While the price of a loaf of rustic bread is the equivalent to 40 subway rides (120元, around US$6.50), the price tags on a pillowy pain au chocolat or a glistening slice of one of the many tarts (the chocolate caramel is the stuff dreams are made of) are less painful to swallow; one forkful and you'll forget you've even paid.

FLASK

A treasure of a bar, if you can find it

432 Shaanxi Nan (South) Lu (near Fuxing Zhong Lu)
陕西南路432号 (近复兴中路) / +86 21 3368 6108
No website / Closed Sunday

This Taiwanese-owned speakeasy, designed by architect Alberto Caiola, is hidden inside a sandwich shop. Once you manage to find the bar's entrance (I'm not going to ruin the surprise for you!), you're rewarded with a sleek space filled with Chesterfield sofas and a mix of metal chairs and leather ottomans-cum-stools. The menu of Prohibition-inspired cocktails is divided into "ladies" and "gents" sections, which seems slightly sexist, but I played along and went for the sweet, but not overly so, Taiwan Plum Soup – osmanthus wine, rum and plum liqueur served in a glass rimmed with plum powder – and was not disappointed.

GINGER BY THE PARK

Worldly eats in a homey space

91 Xingguo Lu (near Hunan Lu) / 兴国路91号 (近湖南路)
+86 21 3406 0599 / gingerfoods.com / Open daily

Located in a three-floor converted house overlooking a teensy park is the aptly named Ginger by the Park, a cozy restaurant with a charming little terrace. The menu features Australian beef and cuisine that spans the Mediterranean, Southeast Asia and Japan, but don't worry – you won't find even a pinch of MSG. Though I consider the portions to be a bit small, everything is well-prepared. I like to start off with the refreshing house-made tofu before digging into the curried pumpkin and cheese croquettes, the spicy pomelo salad and the mentaiko spaghetti, coated in codfish roe and flavored with shiso, which is certainly worth the 20-minute wait.

GOGA

Delightful Californian-Asian fusion

1 Yueyang Lu (near Dongping Lu) / 岳阳路1号 (近东平路)
+86 21 6431 9700 / **gogarestaurants.com** / **Open daily**

Behind plate glass windows is this pint-sized restaurant, named after San Francisco's Golden Gate Bridge. Chef and owner Brad Turley, a California native, worked in Hawaii and Vietnam before making his way to Shanghai, and those stints have influenced his food – think black pork belly from nearby Wuxi served with miso maple bourbon mustard, garlic tuna aioli and arugula with parmesan, or blackened beef tataki with green chili citrus paste, yuzu and ponzu. GoGa has 20-odd seats and fills up quickly, but if it's packed when you arrive, you're in luck: in the building right behind it is Hai by GoGa, a rooftop offshoot with the same menu.

IDLE BEATS

Screen printing at its loudest

115 Pingwu Lu (near Xingfu Lu)
平武路115号 (近幸福路)
+86 139 1867 7786 / idlebeats.com
Closed Monday

China's first independent print art studio was founded by two Shanghai-based artists, Nini Sum and Gregor Koerting. Though the duo also dabble in sculpture and installation art, their shop focuses on translating their color-filled, often neon, aesthetic into illustration and screen printing. They're known in the city for their limited edition posters, and, on a global scale, have created designs for Uniqlo, Vans and Red Bull. Nini and Gregor also run three-hour screen printing workshops for beginners as well as classes for those who are more experienced. So whether you're looking to acquire new skills or a snazzy piece for your wall, this is your one-stop shop.

JIANGUO 328

MSG-free Shanghainese food

328 Jianguo Xi (West) Lu (near Xiangyang Nan (South) Lu)
建国西路328号 (近襄阳南路) / +86 21 6471 3819 / No website
Open daily

Karen Chen dreamed of a restaurant where she could eat classic local dishes and not worry about the ingredients. So she opened one. Chen cooks with filtered water, has banished MSG and banned smoking, a rare treat for Shanghai, where smoking indoors is still common. My pick here is the yellow fish with scallions: five fried yellow Atlantic croakers topped with a mountain of fried scallions. A Shanghainese restaurant isn't one without serving hongshao rou (fatty pork braised in sugar, wine, soy sauce and ginger), and the offering here hits the mark, subbing in delicate quail's eggs for the standard chicken's egg that is served alongside the pork and bathed in its sweet sauce.

LANZHOU LAMIAN

Street-side noodles served around the clock

50 Gao'an Lu (near Hengshan Lu) / 高安路50号 (近衡山路)
No phone or website / Open daily

Lanzhou, a city in northwest China, is famous for its lamian – fresh, hand-pulled noodles. These humble, family-run shops generically called "Lanzhou Lamian" can be found throughout the city, but once you've spied the discerning cabbies pulling up to eat here and have had a taste of the fare, you'll understand why this one is my top lamian spot. To order, point to a photo on the picture menu, and you'll shortly be delivered a steaming bowl of noodles with beef or mutton in a cilantro broth. If you'd prefer a veggie-friendly option, order fanqie chaodan daoxiaomian, which has thick chewy noodles and is topped with tomato and egg.

LA PÉTANQUE

Putting the French back in French Concession

139 Tai'an Lu (near Huashan Lu) / 泰安路139号 (近华山路)
+86 21 6281 4891 / facebook.com/pages/La-Petanque-Shanghai
Closed Monday

From down the block you can hear the thwack of pétanque balls being thrown on the court here, where there's no lack of Europeans playing the game, which is similar to bocce, and sipping Pastis. La Pétanque bills itself as a restaurant, but to me it has more of a bar atmosphere, and, honestly, the drinks are better than the food, though Gallic classics like baby potatoes with brie and garlic prawns do fit the bill after you've worked up a post-game appetite. Happy hour runs 4–8pm daily, and that, along with the pétanque court, is what secured this as one of my regular after-work watering holes.

MADISON

Modern American cuisine

1414 Huaihai Zhong Lu (near Fuxing Xi (West) Lu) / 淮海中路1414号
(近复兴西路) / **+86 21 6437 0136** / madisoninshanghai.com
Closed Monday

After growing up in China, Taiwan and Japan, Madison owner/chef
Austin Hu returned to his home country of the US for school, and
eventually cut his teeth cooking at New York's swanky Gramercy Tavern.
Austin returned to Shanghai, where he had spent his middle school
years, and opened Madison (so-named for the city in Wisconsin where he
attended university). His kitchen turns out attractive plates loaded with
the likes of roasted sea perch with house-made kimchi and sweet potato
ravioli with vinegar from Shanxi province. If you swing by for the ultra-
popular weekend brunch, you'd be remiss not to order the Scotch duck
eggs or the face-sized scone with clotted cream.

OLD JESSE

Taste the city's classics

41 Tianping Lu (near Huaihai Xi (West) Lu) / 天平路41号 (近淮海西路)
+86 21 6282 9260 / No website / Open daily

Despite being a little shabby, with low ceilings, crowded tables and
not much ambiance to speak of, Old Jesse slings traditional dishes to
the eager locals, expats and visiting foodies who flock here every night.
Service is notably bad here, but just accept that and let the food speak
for itself. The hongshao rou, that staple of Shanghainese cuisine, is
fatty, sweet, sticky and made in table-sized portions. I always go for the
flavorful braised fish head topped with fried spring onions, a bowl of
congyou banmian (scallion oil noodles), and tiny river shrimp cooked in
Shaoxing wine.

ORDEN BOWLING CENTRE
More than strikes and spares

3rd Floor, 10 Hengshan Lu (near Gao'an Lu) / 徐汇区衡山路10号3楼 (近高安路) / +86 21 6474 6666 / No website / Open daily

Whether you're a gutter ball expert or a master of the dreaded two pin split, Orden Bowling Centre is the type of place that's fun no matter your skill — or lack thereof. The 16-lane, smoke-free bowling alley is open 24 hours, perfect for when you get the urge for a low-key activity to continue a night out or need to while away a rainy day. But the best part is that Orden also features pool tables, arcade games and even a massage chair, so that if you need a break from throwing a weighted ball down a greased lane, there are plenty of other entertainment options. If you start to feel peckish, there's a snack menu with mainstays like popcorn, ice cream and soda, but if you're thirsty for something more adult, have no fear: there's an entire inebriates menu.

SALUTE

A slice of Italian countryside

59 Fuxing Xi (West) Lu (near Yongfu Lu) / 复兴西路59号 (近永福路)
+86 21 3461 9828 / facebook.com/pages/Salute / Open daily

The shaded courtyard, wooden shelves lined with bottles of wine
and exposed rafters from which hang drying sausages give Salute
a rustic Italian vibe. You can choose to sit in the courtyard or in one
of three adjoining rooms indoors; if cigarette smoke bothers you,
opt for outside. The blackboard menu lists the handful of dishes,
including cold cuts, a cheese plate and Caprese salad, but I can't help
ordering the panini, which is served hot off the grill, and is oozing with
mozzarella, salami and ripe tomatoes. This is a wonderful place to
spend a casual afternoon, so make it a day, pick your poison (wine or
beer), order up and enjoy.

SONGFANG MAISON DE THÉ

Chinese-French tea house

227 Yongjia Lu (near Shaanxi Nan (South) Lu) / 永嘉路227号
(近陕西南路) / **+86 21 6443 8283** / **songfangtea.com** / **Open daily**

Parisian transplant Florence Samson took a 1930s lane house and her passion for luxury goods and turned them into a peaceful place to sip premium teas. Chinese and French teas are sold on the sunny first floor, which is decorated with the shop's signature cornflower blue tea canisters as well as vintage tea tins. Up the wooden staircase is the light-filled café, which serves sweet treats like financiers and chocolate cake, and teas such as China Blue, a white tea blend with coconut, blackberry and orange. I don't recommend you buy Chinese tea here, as the price is quite marked up, but if it's French tea you're after, this is the best shop to find it.

THE AVOCADO LADY

A grocery store for the rest of us

274 Wulumuqi Lu (near Wuyuan Lu) / 乌鲁木齐路274号 (近五原路)
+86 21 6437 7262 / facebook.com/thAvocadoLady / Open daily

As recently as 2008, it was pretty hard to find avocados in Shanghai. So when Jiang Qin started stocking the fateful green fruit at her family-run produce shop, word quickly spread, and she earned a nickname: The Avocado Lady. Customers soon began requesting she stock other imported items — parmesan, kale, San Pellegrino — and The Avocado Lady delivered, selling the goods at a fraction of supermarket prices. Today, The Avocado Lady has gone from fruit slinger to full-on grocer, and her group of loyal patrons continues to grow. I do all my grocery shopping here. Craving a hard-to-find imported food? You'd be smart to pop by and peruse the shelves.

WANLING TEA HOUSE
A traditional Chinese tea shop

No. 1, Lane 619 Jianguo Lu (near Anting Lu) / 建国西路619弄1号
(近安亭路) / +86 135 6424 8308 / wanlingteahouse.com / Open daily

The proprietress of this well-stocked tea shop, Wan Ling, grew up in a tea-growing family. When she and her husband, James (whom she met when he walked into the tea shop where she was working), moved to Shanghai, it only made sense that the two open a tea shop of their own. When I need a hostess gift or just want to inquire about particular teas, I make a beeline for Wanling Tea House, where both owners speak English and are happy to explain the subtle properties of teas like Longjing (dragon well) green tea from nearby Hangzhou. Tastings are available any time, but prices vary and you do need to call ahead to book.

WUJIE

Exquisite Chinese haute cuisine for herbivores

392 Tianping Lu (near Zhaojiabang Lu) / 天平路392号 (近肇嘉浜路)
+86 21 3469 2857 / facebook.com/WUJIERestaurant / Open daily

Wujie is Shanghai's only upscale vegetarian Chinese restaurant, and they haven't cut any corners. The restaurant, covering a massive five floors, doesn't feel enormous when you're inside, and the service is so polished that you'd never even know they were busy. To be environmentally friendly, the menu is listed on an iPad, which is brought to your table, and the dishes change seasonally. The kitchen sources high-quality ingredients from around the country, like organic strawberries from nearby Chongming Island and truffles from Yunnan province. I love the crispy and creamy tofu tempura, with its amalgam of textures, and the sweet, nutty braised chickpeas with broad beans and a pumpkin crêpe.

YI ZHANG HONG (一丈红)

Healthier, cleaner Sichuan eats

356 Wulumuqi Zhong Lu (near Fuxing Xi (West) Lu)
乌鲁木齐中路356号 (近复兴西路) / +86 21 6471 8687
No website / Open daily

At Yi Zhang Hong, it's all about Sichuan fare that's also a little good for you. Though it's unfussy, you'll pay more here than you would in other Sichuan restaurants because of the high quality of the ingredients, particularly the Australian and New Zealand beef. It wouldn't be Sichuan without mapo doufu (tofu in a chili and bean sauce), and the version here uses smoky, firm tofu suspended in chili oil (though if, like me, you prefer standard soft tofu, just ask for it) and served with fish. Chili oil sounds threatening, but even those with a sensitive tongue will be able to nosh on the tender slices of fish and bean sprouts.

SHANGHAI AFTER DARK:
watering holes with character

The finest tipples in town

For a night out in Shanghai, I recommend getting dressed up and going for an upscale bar crawl, so that you can hit up as many of the city's top-notch cocktail joints as possible.

Start at proper speakeasy **Speak Low**, the entrance of which is hidden within a bar supply shop. The main bar is low-lit and intimate, but go one more floor up, figure out how to open the door and you'll find yourself in a lovely secluded area with more seating and a whole other bar. The English Mule, a Moscow Mule made with Earl Grey tea-infused gin, served in the standard copper mug, is sublime.

Walk west on Fuxing Lu and head for **The Union Trading Company**, which is jointly owned by Madison chef Austin Hu (see pg 69) and bartender Yao Lu. There are an astounding 100-odd drinks available: I'm fond of the refreshing Waltzing Matilda, made with gin, white and sparkling wines, passion fruit syrup and lime juice, that Yao says dates from 1895, proving that good taste never goes out of style.

Senator Saloon isn't a speakeasy, but its barely marked entrance belies the warm space within. Priding itself as a whiskey bar, the menu is full of old standbys like Manhattans, Old Fashions and Mint Juleps, as well as twists on traditional tipples, like their sweet Bee's Knees, made with gin, lemon juice and lemongrass-infused honey delivered in a Champagne coupe.

Down the block is lively **el Coctel**, the result of Willy Moreno's desire to bring to Shanghai the kind of bar he frequented in Barcelona. Moreno, known for being zany, says that the room divider made of cocktail shakers is meant to evoke a giant abacus, and the beautiful floral ceiling, painted by artist Veronica Ballart Lilja, is an appealing, unexpected touch. Try the Efficient Ramos Gin Fizz (gin, lime juice, sugar and egg white shaken with orange bitters and seltzer).

Some might call it gaudy, but I love the red bar, blue velvet stools, lavender trim and chartreuse ceiling at **Taste Buds Cocktail Palace**, which is found south of el Coctel. Don't miss the Tale of Mulata, a kicky, concoction of chili-infused rum, lime juice and basil, topped with rose petals and gold flakes, and served in a glass wrapped in imitation US dollar bills that will have you ending your night with a spicy, cheeky bang.

EL COCTEL
2nd Floor, 47 Yongfu Lu (near Fuxing Xi (West) Lu)
永福路47号2号楼 (近复兴西路), +86 21 6433 6511
el-coctel.com, open daily

SENATOR SALOON
98 Wuyuan Lu (near Wulumuqi Lu), 五原路98号
(近乌鲁木齐路), +86 21 5423 1330
senatorsaloon.com open daily

SPEAK LOW
579 Fuxing Zhong Lu (near Ruijin Er Lu), 复兴中路
579号 (近瑞金二路), +86 21 6416 0133, no website
open daily

TASTE BUDS COCKTAIL PALACE
2nd Floor, 368 Wukang Lu (near Hunan Lu), 武康路
368号2号楼 (近湖南路), +86 138 1802 1597
no website, open daily

THE UNION TRADING COMPANY
64 Fenyang Lu (at Fuxing Zhong Lu), 汾阳路64号
(入口在复兴中路), +86 21 6418 3077
facebook.com/pages/The-Union-Trading-Company
closed Sunday

SHANGHAI AFTER DARK:
late night eats

Where to feed your rumbling tum in the wee hours

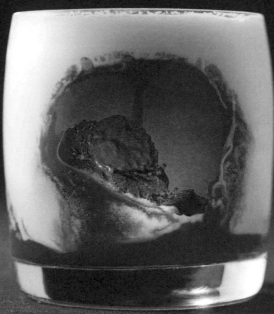

MR & MRS BUND

CHANGLE LU AND SHAANXI NAN (SOUTH) LU

Whether you're a night owl or in need of sopping up the booze before calling it a night, Shanghai's late-night eateries have you covered: here, you'll find everything from street-side noodles to Bund-side scallops.

Closet-sized **Yakitori Fukuchan** grills up its namesake skewers of veggies and meats with sides like fresh tofu topped with bonito flakes. You'll find yourself toasting with sloshing cups of shōchū and wolfing down crispy chicken skin.

For something local, head to the corner of **Changle Lu and Shaanxi Nan (South) Lu**. In warmer weather, street food vendors set up shop starting around 10pm and sling fried rice, fried noodles and skewered meat, seafood, tofu and vegetables (called chuan'r and pronounced "chwar") for the late-night crowd.

Hungry, but not starving? Then you need tapas. Mosey over to **Pirata** (see pg 47) for plates of foie gras toast, house-made chorizo and fragrant spicy clams with Thai basil. It's a rookie mistake to skip dessert here – in fact, you'd be smart to order two.

If you're out on the Bund and peckish, be sure to stop at **Mr & Mrs Bund**. The chicken picnic aioli sounds simple but is in fact a sous-vide chicken breast that's lightly grilled and served with garlic aioli. For those with a sweet tooth, order the lemon and lemon tart. This is a hollowed-out lemon that's been poached, candied and filled with lemon sorbet, lemon curd, slices of orange and grapefruit, and vanilla Chantilly cream.

For a humbler affair within walking distance of the Bund bars, head to **Shouning Lu**, a street lined with stalls selling seafood and tuck into spicy, bright-red crayfish, and grilled scallops and oysters smothered in garlic. Crayfish are sold by the jin (half kilo); for two people, one jin is enough. Be sure to end the meal on a sweet note with grilled bananas.

SHOUNING LU

CHANGLE LU AND SHAANXI NAN (SOUTH) LU
STREET FOOD CORNER
Changle Lu (at Shaanxi Nan (South) Lu), 长乐路
(近陕西南路), no phone or website, open daily

MR & MRS BUND
6th Floor, 18 Zhongshan Dong (East) Yi Lu (near Nanjing
Dong (East) Lu), 中山东一路18号6楼
(近南京东路), +86 21 6323 9898, mmbund.com
open daily

PIRATA
136 Xinle Lu (near Xiangyang Bei (North) Lu)
新乐路136号 (近襄阳北路), +86 21 5404 2327
no website, closed Monday

SHOUNING LU
Shouning Lu (near Xizang Nan (South) Lu), 寿宁路
(近西藏南路), no phone or website, open daily

YAKITORI FUKUCHAN
223 Changle Lu (near Shaanxi Nan (South) Lu)
长乐路223号 (近陕西南路), +86 21 5403 6270
no website, open daily

PIRATA

tianzifang

A labyrinth of narrow laneways lined with brick houses, Tianzifang dates from the 1930s. As the neighborhood has grown, its name has come to encompass both the laneways as well as the main road, Taikang Lu. When families moved out, artists moved in, setting up studios here in the historic stone gatehouses, called shikumen. From 2005, the area slowly began developing into a trendy, creative hive of shops and businesses. Today, Tianzifang can be jam-packed with tourists and often busy on weekends, but the area has retained some authenticity, with low-hanging power lines and streets lined with red lanterns. The surrounding roads are as quiet as Tianzifang is hectic, and perfect for strolling when you need to take a break from the crowd.

1 Kaiba Tap House
2 Liuli China Museum
3 Old China Hand Reading Room

4 Platane
5 Vienna Café
6 Zhou Enlai's House

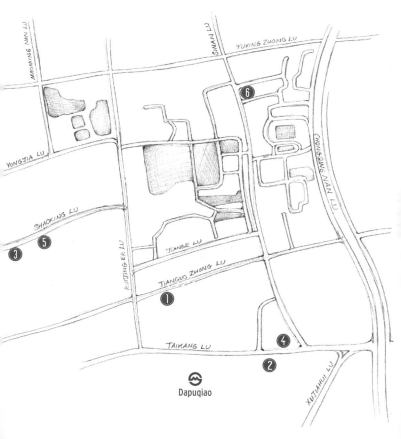

KAIBA TAP HOUSE

Beer all the way from Belgium

2nd Floor, Taikang Terrace, 169 Jianguo Zhong Lu (near Ruijin Er Lu)
建国中路169号2楼（近瑞金二路）/ +86 21 6418 2252 / kaiba-beerbar.com
Open daily

Chinese beer is cheap (yay!) but weak (boo!), which makes Kaiba Tap House all the more welcome in Shanghai. The laid-back bar has a wide range of Belgian brews on tap and, if you're unfamiliar with the selection, the staff is happy to pour a sample, so you can be well-informed when you order. Food is standard pub fare – burgers and fries, pizza, fried calamari – and will fill your belly. There's also a small patio overlooking the narrow residential laneway, perfect for when you want a bit of fresh air. For an unbeatable happy hour with great deals on imported pints, you can't go wrong here.

LIULI CHINA MUSEUM

Stunning glass art

25 Taikang Lu (near Sinan Lu) / 泰康路25号（近似南路）
+86 21 6467 2268 / liulichinamuseum.com / Open daily

This was Shanghai's first glass museum and even though there's now the superb Shanghai Museum of Glass in Baoshan district, the Liuli China Museum remains my favorite. The striking exterior is made of 12,000 glass bricks, which allow the shop and café to be flooded with light. The museum has a beautiful permanent collection and holds regular exhibitions, often featuring international artists. Past exhibitors have included Paul Stankard, whose work has been shown at New York's Metropolitan Museum of Art, Anne Wolff, who has pieces housed at Los Angeles County Museum of Art, and Liuligonfang founder and art director Loretta Hui-shan Yang, who has also exhibited at the Victoria & Albert Museum in London. Plus, it's just so pretty.

OLD CHINA HAND
READING ROOM

A hideaway for book lovers

**27 Shaoxing Lu (near Shaanxi Nan (South) Lu) / 绍兴路27
(近陕西南路) / +86 21 6473 2526 / han-yuan.com / Open daily**

I like to come to this library and café, the brainchild of photographer
Deke Ehr and Tess Johnston (the namesake Old China Hand), when the
weather is frightful and curl up with one of the English-language books
about Shanghai published by Old China Hand Press. The space is bright,
furnished with antique pieces, including a piano, and filled with books,
making this heaven for bibliophiles. With free Wi-Fi it's a fantastic place
to get work done, or to get lost in a good book.

PLATANE

French influenced contemporary home goods

156 Taikang Lu (near Sinan Lu) 泰康路156号 (近似南路)
+86 21 6466 2495 / platane.cn / Open daily

Owner Laetitia Charachon moved to Shanghai in 2004 and opened up Platane, bridging the gap between Eastern and Western interior design styles. The airy shop stocks lovely ceramics and décor such as light fixtures and textiles, and regularly partners with well-known designers for exclusive, limited edition collections. I love the blue and white dinnerware set designed by French artist Nathalie Vialars. Cast in Jingdezhen, China's porcelain capital, these appear at first glance to look like traditional blue-and-white Chinese pottery, but upon closer examination you'll find that the blue used here is much bolder.

VIENNA CAFÉ

Bright, comfortable coffee house

No. 2, 25 Shaoxing Lu (near Shaanxi Nan (South) Lu) / 绍兴路25弄2号 (近陕西南路) / +86 21 6445 2131 / No website / Open daily

On tranquil, tree-lined Shaoxing Lu you'll find Vienna Café, a wonderful place to take a break after pottering around the area. Owned by an Austrian expat, the space features crisp striped wallpaper, dark wood wainscoting and a polished hardwood floor. Sunlight pours in through the atrium, providing the pleasant sense of being outside without the sweltering heat. This coffee shop has a homey, inviting atmosphere that will have you rearranging your day so that you can settle in and spend a lazy afternoon here, sipping coffee and leisurely snacking on a thick slice of homemade apple and plum cake.

ZHOU ENLAI'S HOUSE

A home with history

73 Sinan Lu (near Fuxing Zhong Lu) / 思南路73号 (近复兴中路)
+86 21 6473 0420 / No website / Open daily

Even if you have limited interest in Chinese history, the former residence of the first Premier of the People's Republic of China is worth a visit. Zhou Enlai lived here with his cronies in the mid-1940s as the battle for China between the Communists and the Kuomintang raged. Built in the 1920s, it's an impressive French-style, three-story home with red trim and ivy growing up the outside. Inside, the dark wooden floors and banisters gleam; the rooms are spartan and have been preserved with the original furnishings, with Zhou's containing nothing more than a narrow iron bed. Whenever I walk through this house, which really has great bones, I can't help but relish the irony of the fact that the then-leader of the very anti-Western Communist Party lived in such a beautiful French home.

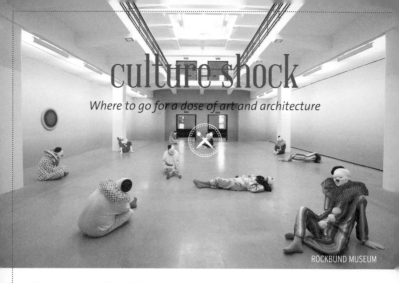

culture shock

Where to go for a dose of art and architecture

ROCKBUND MUSEUM

The art scene in Shanghai is booming. It seems there are museums and galleries in every neighborhood, featuring art of every media, which means that no matter where you find yourself, you have the opportunity to take in a bit of art. So, break up eating, drinking and shopping with stops at Shanghai's most compelling galleries and museums.

Ming Ming Chen and Jeff Zhou's immaculate **Around Space Gallery** lives in a gorgeous, if slightly crumbling, 1930s Art Deco building near the Bund. The gallery represents and displays the works of 40 artists; the pieces that have struck my fancy most come from multi-disciplinary Shanghainese artist Maleonn, who travels with his mobile studio and photographs people dressed in whimsical costumes.

When you're in the French Concession, pop by Martin Kemble's **Art Labor Gallery** where half of the artists whose work is shown are a mixed bag of foreigners, including *Generation X* author Douglas Coupland, whose solo show of paintings was held here. The other half are Chinese, like Lu Xinjian, whose *City DNA* series I dream of hanging in my future home.

MAGDA DANYSZ GALLERY

At **Magda Danysz Gallery** the eponymous owner's massive pull in the art world brings in the work of big names like street artists JR, Miss Van and JonOne, Liu Bolin's *Hiding in the City* series and works by French photographer Alain Delorme, known for his colorful photos of huge loads being carted by bicycle around Shanghai.

Photography is the name of the game at **M97 Gallery**, much of it in black and white. The gallery does represent photographers who work in striking color, though, such as Michael Wolf, whose moody snaps of major metropolises, as seen in his series *Tokyo Compression* and *Architecture of Density*, are mesmerizing.

Housed in a 1930s former bank building on Suzhou Creek, **OCT Contemporary Art Terminal** (OCAT), is a non-profit contemporary art organization. Most solo shows are from Chinese artists, but past major shows have included an exhibition by esteemed cinematographer/photographer Yang Fudong and group animation show *The Garden of Forking Paths*.

The privately owned **Rockbund Museum** has no permanent collection, and instead hosts rotating exhibitions. They've mounted shows by Chinese heavy-hitters Zhang Huan and Cai Guo-Qiang, as well as work by foreign artists. Like most buildings along the Bund, you can access the roof to spend some time enjoying the sights while sipping the cup of coffee or tea that is included in admission.

At Bund-side **Long Museum** you can admire the impressive collection of billionaire couple Liu Yiqian and Wang Wei as well as rotating exhibits. These are often China-centric – for example, the museum has shown a selection of Qing dynasty paintings and mounted an exhibition of propaganda-era revolutionary art, but they do sometimes veer into unexpected territory, like an exhibition on the history of Mexican silver.

Being a real estate voyeur, I was beyond delighted when I found the **Shikumen Open House Museum**, a model of a stone gatehouse, in Xintiandi. Built around a common courtyard, these were once the most popular style of housing you'd find in Shanghai, but most were razed to make way for shops and restaurants. This museum is a marvelous way to do a little time traveling and see how people once lived in these grand homes.

AROUND SPACE GALLERY
No. 703, 33 Sichuan Zhong Lu (near Guangdong Lu)
四川中路33号703室 (近广东路), +86 21 3305 0100
aroundspace.gallery, closed Monday

ART LABOR GALLERY
Inside Surpass Court, 570 Yongjia Lu (near Yueyang Lu)
永嘉路570号 (近岳阳路), +86 21 3460 5331
artlaborgallery.com, closed Monday

LONG MUSEUM
3398 Longteng Da Dao (near Ruining Lu)
龙腾大道3398号 (近瑞宁路), +86 21 6422 7636
thelongmuseum.org, closed Monday

M97 GALLERY
2nd Floor, 97 Moganshan Lu (near Changhua Lu)
莫干山路97号2楼 (近昌化路), +86 21 6266 1597
m97gallery.com, closed Sunday and Monday

MAGDA DANYSZ GALLERY
188 Linqing Lu (near Yangshupu Lu)
临青路188号 (近杨树浦路), +86 21 5513 9599
magda-gallery.com, closed Monday

OCT CONTEMPORARY ART TERMINAL
1016 Suzhou Bei (North) Lu (near Wen'an Lu)
北苏州路1016号 (近文安路), +86 21 6608 5180
ocatshanghai.com, closed Monday

ROCKBUND MUSEUM
20 Huqiu Lu (near Beijing Dong (East) Lu)
虎丘路20号 (近北京东路), +86 21 3310 9985
rockbundartmuseum.org/en, closed Monday

SHIKUMEN OPEN HOUSE MUSEUM
No. 25, 181 Taikang Lu (near Madang Lu)
太仓路181弄25号 (近马当路), +86 21 3307 0337
shanghaixintiandi.com, open daily

OCT CONTEMPORARY ART TERMINAL

xintiandi

Xintiandi, meaning "new heaven and earth," is the name of a complex of restored shikumen (stone gatehouses) that were once homes but are now shops, restaurants and bars, as well as the surrounding area. The neighborhood is sandwiched between Huaihai Zhong Lu, one of Shanghai's high streets that boasts lots of stores you'll recognize from any mall you've been to, and Fuxing Lu, which is quite staid in comparison. Xintiandi proper is touristy and expensive, but beyond this enclave for the nouveau riche is a truly local enclave: many traditional lane complexes remain and you'll still find folks chatting in their pajamas, fruit sellers hawking their produce and kids running around pantless and giggling.

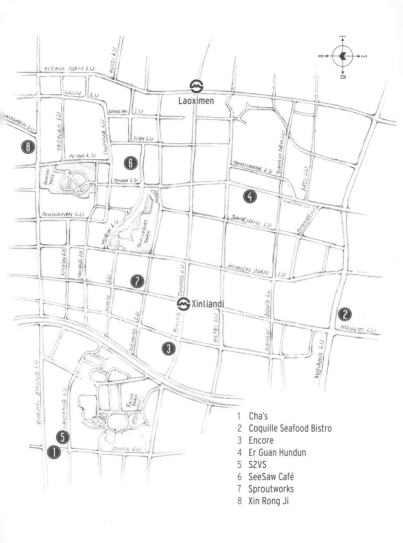

1 Cha's
2 Coquille Seafood Bistro
3 Encore
4 Er Guan Hundun
5 S2VS
6 SeeSaw Café
7 Sproutworks
8 Xin Rong Ji

CHA'S

Throwback Hong Kong dining

30 Sinan Lu (near Huaihai Zhong Lu) / 思南路30号 (近淮海中路)
+86 21 6093 2062 / Open daily

This detailed recreation of a 1950s cha chaan teng (Hong Kong diner)
is chock-full of items that will have Hong Kongers waxing nostalgic.
The place is properly outfitted: it's got a vintage cooler stocked with glass
bottles of soda, stained-glass partitions, a rotary phone and a just-slightly-
worn green-and-white tile floor. After many meals here with friends in
the know, I feel up to the task of recommending what they would order:
milk tea or boiled Coca-Cola with ginger to imbibe while you tuck into
poached chicken, beef brisket, egg fried rice, broccoli stir-fried with garlic
and boluobao (pineapple buns). The only downside is that the prices aren't
what they were in the '50s – that said, they're still pretty low.

COQUILLE SEAFOOD BISTRO

French fine dining

29 Mengzi Lu (near Xujiahui Lu) / 蒙自路29号 (近徐家汇路)
+86 21 3376 8127 / **facebook.com/coquille.scarpetta** / **Closed Monday**

Banker-turned-restaurateur John Liu's brasserie, which is actually a few blocks south of Xintiandi, but close enough that it's not too far out of the way, is popular for good reason. Seafood is tops here — as it should be for a restaurant named "coquille", meaning "shell" in French — though it can be pricey. I tend to go straight for the escargot, imported from France and swimming in a heavenly mix of lemongrass-ginger butter, kaffir lime and coriander. A treat, too, are mussels from Australia. Not a seafood fan? There's rich duck confit served with a hearty butterbean cassoulet and, to finish you off, pork cracklings.

ENCORE

Affordable drinks in a swanky neighborhood

468 Fuxing Zhong Lu (near Danshui Lu) / 复兴中路468号 (近淡水路)
+86 158 0182 1027 / No website / Open daily

This upscale cocktail bar lives inside a heritage building, where the ornate plaster ceiling has been lovingly restored. Coupled with the dark wood paneling, low lighting, a disused fireplace and small outdoor patio, this spot is full of a cozy, comfortable ambiance. The drinks menu is arranged by flavor profile (e.g., bitter, smoky, umami), and the tipples are made in the Prohibition style. I usually pop in here for the buy-one-get-one-free happy hour that runs from 5pm to 8pm and order Encore's twist on the Moscow Mule, named for actor Nicholas Tse; it's got vodka, fresh lemon and ginger, apple juice and lapsang souchong syrup. Bottoms up!

ER GUAN HUNDUN

Late-night street eats

209-213 Zhaozhou Lu (near Hefei Lu) / 肇周路209-213号 (近合肥路)
No phone or website / Open daily

Judging by the anticipatory queue that forms outside Er Guan Hundun before the stove's even been lit, the Pang family know what they're doing. The wontons with pork and mustard greens sold here are tender, meaty and made even better by the peanut sauce served on the side. In addition to the wontons, there are deep fried boneless pork chops, which aren't to be missed. During the warmer months, a few tables are set up outside, but know that these go quickly. If they're taken, you can always eat indoors or, if you're lucky, a local family might invite you to sit with them. Be sure to toast them with a bottle of Tsingtao (pronounced "Qingdao") beer and then get to chowing down.

S2VS

Modern threads for gents

172 Nanchang Lu (near Sinan Lu) / 南昌路172号 (近似南路)
+86 21 6333 7057 / s2vs.com / Open daily

After graduating from Parsons School of Design, Indonesian expat
Sean William Salim – whose initials create S2VS (the two Vs making a W) –
stayed in New York and started his menswear line there, but it's Shanghai
where he decided to set up shop. Housed on one of the city's most verdant
streets, the narrow boutique is filled with stylish menswear that errs on
the side of prep. I love the soft T-shirts, the charcoal gray wool bomber
jacket with wooden buttons, the fun Kelly green shorts embroidered with
tiny alligators and the handsome blue suede bucks with teal laces that
provide an unexpected pop of color.

SEESAW CAFÉ

Quality coffee in a caffeine desert

150 Hubin Lu (near Jinan Lu) 湖滨路150号（近济南路）
+86 21 6333 0770   facebook.com/SeesawCoffee
Closed Saturday and Sunday

SeeSaw Café's baristas are proud coffee geeks, and this was evident the first time I watched them prepare my smooth cappuccino. Choose your coffee type – think latte, cappuccino, single-origin pour – and then choose how it's prepared (with a syphon, a hand-press or standard). Beans come from all over; on one visit, I had an Americano made with Indonesian java and, on another, with grounds from Kenya. This outpost of SeeSaw is open to the lobby of an office building (the other location is in Jing'an), but don't let that deter you; you won't find a better cup of coffee in Xintiandi.

SPROUTWORKS

For when you can't stomach another dumpling

185 Madang Lu (near Zizhong Lu) / 马当路185号 (近自忠路)
+86 21 6339 0586 / sproutworks.com.cn / Open daily

Living in China has its perks: tasty Chinese food (or is it just food here?) is everywhere and it's easy to go overboard. So when visiting friends have overdosed on local food and need a break, I take them to Sproutworks, which sells paninis and wraps, soups, salads and side dishes that change daily. Pro tip: go for the sides, which are moreish and inexpensive. Four sides – think spicy roasted cauliflower with mint and feta; wild rice with cranberries, pecans and Mandarin oranges; kale, mango and pepitas – are filling, but won't leave you rolling home.

XIN RONG JI

Mouth-watering dim sum

5th Floor Shanghai Plaza, 138 Huaihai Zhong Lu (near Longmen Lu)
淮海中路138号5楼 (近龙门路) / **+86 21 5386 5757 / No website**
Open daily

I started coming here for dim sum simply because it's across from my gym and I'm always ravenous after a workout. The problem is, now it's part of my gym routine. I've never sat down to eat here without ordering xia jiao (shrimp dumplings), XO luobogao (turnip cake fried with spicy XO sauce) and mifen (fried rice vermicelli, served here with strips of tofu, egg, shrimp and shredded vegetables). For greens, my pick is always sijidou, dry-fried green beans with garlic. The dim sum menu is in Chinese, but if you tell your server the names of things you like, they'll put in your order and you'll be inhaling your meal in no time.

bao down

Where to go for iconic xiaolongbao and shengjianbao

Welcome to Shanghai, home of delicious dumplings of all types. Xiaolongbao (小笼包) are thin-skinned, steamed dumplings filled with meat – most often pork – and brothy, flavorful soup that, for those who aren't practiced, will end up being a delicious mess if you're not careful to use the Chinese spoon in concert with the chopsticks. Shengjianbao (生煎包), on the other hand, are the pillowy, crispy-on-the-bottom cousins of xiaolongbao, are also filled with broth, but are thick and greasy in the most indulgent way.

In a clean and semi-air-conditioned space, **Xiao Yang's Shengjian** slings plastic plates (or Styrofoam takeaway containers) of shengjianbao. You can order the original pork or the shrimp, with regular or black sesame seeds. They come four to an order – more than enough for one person who also plans to eat xiaolongbao across the street – so if you decide to swing by here, bring a big appetite.

Directly across the street, taunting you as you resist shoveling in your second shengjianbao, is **Jia Jia Tang Bao**, which will almost certainly have a queue. The menu of xiaolongbao is in Mandarin only and it's a little grubby in there, but don't let that deter you. The most popular fillings are pork, crab and a combination of the two; if you're having trouble telling them apart, pork will be the least expensive and crab the most.

ZUN KE LAI

On the other side of town at **Fu Chun**, it's much the same: slightly sticky floor, menu in Chinese, queue out the door. Take a number, order when you're called and then wait for stools to open up. You'll make new friends sitting at the shared tables, and they'll laugh good-naturedly at you as you try to eat your xiaolongbao without spraying soup everywhere (then they'll hand you a napkin).

There's no English sign at **Zun Ke Lai**, so look instead for the words "Honored Guest Coming". The poster-size menu, all in Mandarin, looks intimidating, but just remember the word "xiaolongbao" and you'll be fine. At six to a basket, they won't leave you in a food coma, so order the crab and pork (their signature) and, if you're still hungry, the plain pork, too.

the bund

South Bund, West Bund

———◦———

Meaning "embankment", the Bund (or Waitan in
Chinese) is an architecture-rich neighborhood that
stands along the west bank of the Huangpu River.
The center of Shanghai's booming trade in the
mid-1800s, thousands of ships floated in and out
of the harbor ferrying tea, furniture, opium and
weapons between East and West. Along the Bund,
both local banks and institutions from Europe and
Hong Kong built grand offices and these Colonial-
style buildings remain today, though now they're
filled with restaurants and bars. Having seen
the success of Bund-side business, the Shanghai
government has developed the land farther south
along the river into what's now being called the
South Bund and West Bund, with the anchor tenants
being the Long Museum and Power Station of Art,
two swish art destinations.

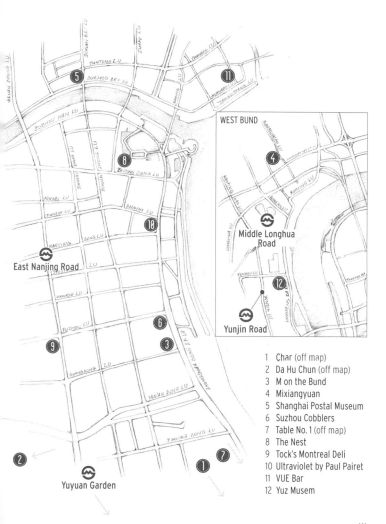

WEST BUND

Middle Longhua Road

Yunjin Road

East Nanjing Road

Yuyuan Garden

1 Char (off map)
2 Da Hu Chun (off map)
3 M on the Bund
4 Mixiangyuan
5 Shanghai Postal Museum
6 Suzhou Cobblers
7 Table No. 1 (off map)
8 The Nest
9 Tock's Montreal Deli
10 Ultraviolet by Paul Pairet
11 VUE Bar
12 Yuz Musem

CHAR

Steak with a side of skyline

29th–31st Floors Hotel Indigo, 585 Zhongshan Dong (East) Er Lu (near Dongmen Lu) / 中山东二路585号29–31楼 (近东门路) +86 21 3302 9995 / char-thebund.com / Open daily

Char is the in-house restaurant at sleek and trendy Hotel Indigo, which sits right on the water's edge. From the roof, the Pudong cityscape is so close it feels like you could reach out and touch it. I'm not big on steak, but I like to drink here because it comes with one of the most stunning views of the city. If you're flush and want to splash out, book in for dinner: Char's chefs take gluttony seriously. The Wagyu eye-fillet beef comes from an environmentally sustainable ranch in Australia and is served with lobster, foie gras, black truffles and wild mushrooms.

DA HU CHUN

Scrumptious dumplings

71 Yunnan Nan (South) Lu (near Jinling Dong (East) Lu)
云南南路71号 (近金陵东路) / **+86 21 6249 3683** / **No website**
Open daily

Shengjianbao are a Shanghai icon. But these dumplings aren't what you're used to: they're half-pan-fried and half thick, doughy bun, so you get both a nice crunch and a nice chew, plus the juicy, meaty pork, or a combo of pork and shrimp, that lives within the confines of the bao. It's always a smart move to patronize Da Hu Chun, where the four shengjianbao you receive with one order are heavenly, but they also do quite nicely as a pre-drinking stomach liner if you have a big night of bar hopping planned. If you want more dumpling recommendations in areas throughout the city, check out the Bao Down feature (see pg 108) for more shengjianbao as well as xiaolongbao hawkers.

M ON THE BUND

Afternoon tea with a priceless view

7th Floor Five on the Bund, 20 Guangdong Lu (near the Bund)
广东路20号外滩5号7楼 (近外滩) / **+86 21 6350 9988**
m-restaurantgroup.com/mbund / Open daily

Successful businesses on the Bund really owe it to Michelle Garnaut; when she opened this restaurant inside a 1921 heritage building in the late '90s, she set the stage for the nightlife explosion that would come a decade later. M on the Bund serves modern pan-European cuisine in an elegant dining room that lets the views do the talking. On the menu are such tasty dishes as the Moroccan modern, a mix of heirloom carrots, chickpeas, cinnamon oranges, sumac and spices, served with an orange blossom dressing and a chickpea flatbread. For my money, though, I come for afternoon tea, as I can't resist a well-made buttery scone.

MIXIANGYUAN

Get your lunch on

1st Floor, 608 Xiaomuqiao Lu (near Zhongshan Nan (South) Er Lu)
小木桥路608号1楼 (近中山南二路) / **+86 21 3366 4408 / No website**
Open daily

In the same building as local restaurateur Anthony Zhao's hot pot restaurant Holy Cow is his cheap and cheerful Shanghainese restaurant. It gets packed every day at lunch by office workers who pour out of the surrounding towers, so it might behoove you to plan an early or slightly later lunch if you want to avoid the rush. The most popular order is lu rou fan (braised pork rice), and for good reason. Tender pork is sliced into juicy slivers and cooked with sautéed shallots, then served on rice and topped with sliced green onion, sweet pickles and Taiwanese pork floss. At lunch, it's part of a set that includes soup, sautéed vegetables, sliced fruit and barley tea, all of which will fill you up until dinner.

SHANGHAI POSTAL MUSEUM

The grandest mailbox in China

**395 Tiantong Lu (near Sichuan Bei (North) Lu) / 天潼路395号
(近四川北路) / +86 21 6393 6666 / No website / Open daily**

This small museum is appropriately housed in Shanghai's former
General Post Office, an imposing Classical-style building that opened in
1924. The exterior features Corinthian columns and a handsome Baroque-
style clock tower, the sides of which have statues of Greek gods Hermes,
Eros and Aphrodite, all of whom are apropos, if a bit cheeky, for a historic
post office. Light pours into the glass atrium where the exhibits are set
up, and it's here where you can learn about the history of China's postal
service. This may sound a little boring, but I promise it's worth a quick look,
and you get to ogle the interior of this gorgeous building. The best bit,
though, is the building's roof, where you can view the entire skyline.

SUZHOU COBBLERS

Luxurious slippers

17 Fuzhou Lu (near the Bund)　福州路17号 (近外滩)
+86 21 6321 7087 suzhou-cobblers.com　Open daily

More than a decade ago, when this neighborhood was still years away
from becoming the hot spot it is now, Denise Lai saw this storefront
for rent and had the good sense to snap it up. Denise began designing
100% silk slippers in 1998, after looking for slippers like the ones her
grandmother once wore, and finding none. After they became a hit, Denise
expanded her line to include silk shoes in a riot of colors for both men and
women. These are the highest quality silk slippers I've found in Shanghai:
I'm particularly fond of the Mary Janes, which are especially sweet.

TABLE NO. 1

Chic continental cuisine

1-3 Maojiayuan Lu (near Waima Lu) / 毛家园路1-3号 (近外马路)
+86 21 6080 2918 / tableno-1.com / Open daily

Helmed by American Christopher Pitts, this restaurant, nestled inside
The Waterhouse at South Bund (see pg 8) has the same look as the rest
of the hotel – concrete, rough-hewn wooden tables, exposed beams and
floor-to-ceiling windows that face the street and courtyard. All plates are
meant to be shared, ideal in a restaurant where you'll want to try a bite
or three of everything. The small menu changes seasonally, so in summer
I might tuck into lentil croquettes with sour cream and watercress while,
come winter, you'll always find me with a spoonful of tuna tartar with
avocado and ponzu.

THE NEST

Not your average Bund bar

6th Floor, 130 Beijing Dong (East) Lu (near Huqiu Lu)
北京东路130号6号楼 (近虎丘路) / **+86 21 6308 7669**
facebook.com/THENESTshanghai / Open daily

An abstract neon light installation hangs above the bar at this stylish watering hole, where it's not trance and house music blasting at an ear-splitting volume but the alt-rock sounds of The Flaming Lips. This is a most welcome departure from every other lounge on the Bund and why I find myself here for birthday parties every other weekend. Vodka is my liquor of choice here, and I like it most in the Birds of Hermes, a fun take on a Bloody Mary with pepper-infused vodka, herbs and a tomato and celery maceration.

TOCK'S MONTREAL DELI

Sandwiches and pickles and poutine, oh my!

221 Henan Zhong Lu (near Fuzhou Lu)
河南中路221号（近福州路）
+86 21 6346 3735 / tocksdeli.com.cn
Open daily

Tock's Montreal Deli is where I go when I need a taste of home, even though I'm a native New Yorker and Tock's hails from Canada. They smoke their meats in-house, and it's for this — thick slices of pastrami sandwiched between rye bread, served with coleslaw and fries — that people flock here. Beyond the meaty sandwiches, I particularly like the matzoh ball soup, another little reminder of NYC for me, and the house-made pickled tomatoes and peppers. It should be noted that this is also one of just a couple of restaurants in the city serving poutine (fries topped with cheese curds and gravy), which is ultra-popular here as a hangover food.

ULTRAVIOLET BY PAUL PAIRET

The ultimate sensory dining experience

Pick up point: 18 Zhongshan Nan (South) Yi Lu (near Nanjing Dong (East) Lu) / 中山南一路18号 (近南京东路)
No phone / uvbypp.cc/bookings / Open daily

Ultraviolet by Paul Pairet epitomizes the phrase "seeing is believing," for until you're sitting in this dining room – a theater, really – you can't imagine that the walls, which are actually video screens, will transform into a forest. This is Shanghai's most exclusive restaurant: the location is a secret – the 10 diners permitted for the night take a bus from Mr & Mrs Bund (see pg 85), and once they arrive, they enjoy 20 courses at 4,000元 (around US$600) per person. Each course has an accompanying sound, sight and smell, all of which are always thematic, but humorously so. For example, dinner kicks off with "Ostie," a frozen apple juice and wasabi sorbet cut into the shape of a Communion wafer. The scent? "Church," customized by perfumer Mane. The visual? Candles and swinging church bells. And on the stereo, what else but AC/DC's "Hells Bells"?

VUE BAR

Sweeping sights and a hot tub

32nd-33rd Floors Hyatt on the Bund, 199 Huangpu Lu (near Wuchang Lu)
黄浦路199号, 32-33楼 (近武昌路) / +86 21 6393 1234
shanghai.bund.hyatt.com/en/hotel/dining/VueBar.html / Open daily

Normally I wouldn't send anyone to a hotel bar, but the view from the
aptly named VUE Bar, which sits atop The Hyatt, is undeniably fantastic,
and worth the 100元 (around US$15) cover charge: don't worry, the price
includes a drink. Sitting at the curve of the Huangpu River, you can see
the Bund's historic buildings on one side of the water and the modern
Pudong skyline on the other, leaving you feeling like a wealthy merchant
surveying your kingdom as you sip. The upper level has an expansive terrace
complete with a Jacuzzi, for those of you willing to don a swimsuit at a bar.
But be sure to get there before 11pm, though, as that's when the lights are
turned off.

YUZ MUSEUM

High-flying art space

35 Fenggu Lu (near Longteng Da Dao)
丰谷路35号（近龙腾大道）
+86 21 6426 1901
yuzmshanghai.org / Closed Monday

A former airport hangar is the grand
setting for this contemporary art
museum, set up by philanthropist
and collector Budi Tek. The massive
venue hosts rotating exhibitions, and
the museum has managed to pull in
some big names such as Yayoi Kusama
and Maurizio Cattelan. Because the
space is so large, installation works are
prominently featured. I was particularly
fond of Hui Li's futuristic *Cage*, made with
green laser beams and a fog machine.
There's also a pleasant, sun-filled café
here, the only one in the still-growing
West Bund area that's worth a visit.

offbeat tours

See a different side of Shanghai

While prepackaged tours are often inauthentic, there are some truly great ones to be found in Shanghai. Led by a local expert, these tours are an informative, fun way to get both your bearings and an introduction to the city.

The White Russians in Shanghai tour run by **Bespoke Travel Company** looks at the rich and sometimes salacious history of those who fled the Bolshevik Revolution and sought refuge in Shanghai during the city's Golden Age. Led by a Siberian photojournalist, the three-hour walking tour is intimate, as it only accommodates up to six. The tour begins in Fuxing Park and takes you back in time with a guided stroll through the streets of the French Concession.

SHANGHAI INSIDERS

Another cultural tour is Israeli photojournalist Dvir Ben-Gal's half-day long **Shanghai Jewish** walking tour. You'll trace the history of Jews in Shanghai, from the small population in the mid-1800s to the boom between 1933 and 1941, when European Jews were fleeing Nazi Germany, and see sites such as the Ohel Moishe Synagogue and the Peace Hotel.

If you prefer your history be learned with the wind in your hair, check out **Shanghai Insiders.** Seated on a motorcycle, either behind the English-speaking driver or in the sidecar, you'll cruise the backstreets of several neighborhoods based on the custom theme of your choosing (options include Art Deco, French Concession, old vs. new).

BESPOKE TRAVEL COMPANY
366 Julu Lu (near Fumin Lu)
巨鹿路 366 (近富民路), +86 136 8314 8453
bespoketravelcompany.com, open daily

CONTEXT TRAVEL
+1 800 691 6036, contexttravel.com, open daily

SHANGHAI INSIDERS
88 Songshan Lu (near Taicang Lu), 嵩山路88号上海
安达仕酒店1楼 (近太仓路), +86 138 1761 6975
shanghaiinsiders.com, open daily

SHANGHAI JEWISH
Shang-Mira Garden Villa No. 1, 89 Shui Chen Nan
(South) Lu (near Hongqiao Lu), 尚米拉花园别墅1,
89水陈楠路 (近虹桥路), +86 130 0214 6702
www.shanghai-Jews.com, open daily

UNTOUR SHANGHAI
No phone, untourshanghai.com, open Monday
and Thursday

UnTour Shanghai does a night markets tour on Monday and Thursday nights, which offers insight into street food culture. You'll head to two markets: one where you'll eat seafood and kebabs, and the other where you can nosh on hand-pulled noodles, sautéed vegetables and fried rice. While tucking in, the guide will give you the low-down on Shanghai street eats.

For a more epicurean experience, check out **Context Travel**'s annotated dinner, a guided meal in which you'll learn the ins and outs of Shanghainese food. The "tour" is led by local food writers and takes place at Jianguo 328 (see pg 66), where you'll taste and learn about authentic Shanghainese dishes. Informative and delectable!